The Night Before Christmas... The Gift

story by Linda Crosland
art by Malcolm Crosland
a Butterfly Promise Book

Butterfly Promise Books is an imprint of
Crosland HILL Publishing, LLC,
25807 Lewis Ranch Road, New Braunfels, TX 78132.
Text copyright © 2007 by Linda Crosland
Illustrations copyright © 2011 by Malcolm Crosland

Scripture quotation from The New Living Translation Holy Bible
Tyndale House Publishers

For more information about Butterfly Promise Books please visit
our website at: croslandhill.com

Designed by Crosland HILL Publishing

Made in the United States of America

Visit the author's website at: lindacrosland.com

Library of Congress Cataloging-in-Publication
Data is available.

ISBN 978-0-9897245-0-0

Dedicated to Aaron and Lane,
two firstborn sons,
and to every reader of
the greatest story ever told....
For God loved the world so much
that he gave his one and only Son,
so that everyone who believes in him
will not perish but have eternal life.
John 3:16 NLT

'Twas the night before Christmas
And all through the town
Not a room to be had
To lay their heads down

For Joseph and Mary
Had come from their
home
To be counted by Caesar
The ruler of Rome

No
Rooms

He didn't care
How difficult it was
Or how far they had come
None would plead their cause

And poor little Mary
About to give birth
To the Son of God
Who was coming to
earth

They finally found a place
In a dark and smelly stable
And made a bed for Him
As best as they were able

Through the night she
labored
Till the King of Kings
was born
The Son of God, Emmanuel
Made it Christmas morn!

For this is what Christmas
is all about
Not lights or food or a
jolly old elf
But a God who reached
down from Heaven
To give us even Himself

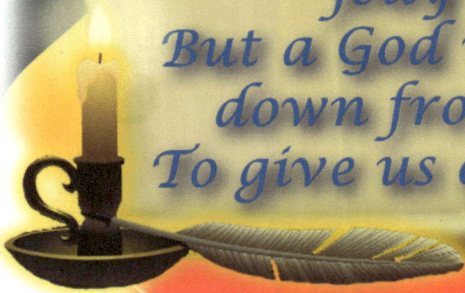

He went straight to work
Touching both shepherds
and kings
That is why angels rejoice
That is why the angel sings

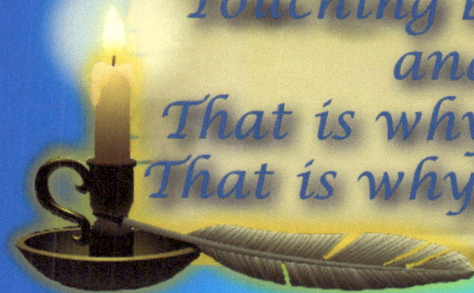

Glory to God in the
highest
Peace goodwill to men
Was there ever such a gift
as this
Unselfish, giving, to the
end?

God, bridging the gap
That sin had made
Through a tiny child who
Was in a manger laid

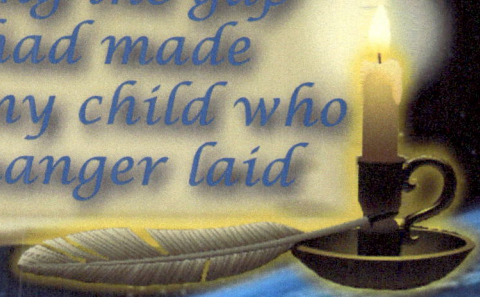

The child who would one day
Lay down His life
To bring us salvation
To give us new life

This gift, wrapped in a
perfect package
Given to everyone you've
met
But hard to believe there
are those
Who haven't opened it yet

They let this gift sit on a shelf
Not dreaming how much it is worth
Not knowing that all their sins
Could be erased by this lowly birth

But wise men still seek Him
In the manger and on the cross
He gives sweet meaning to our lives
He is the way home for the lost

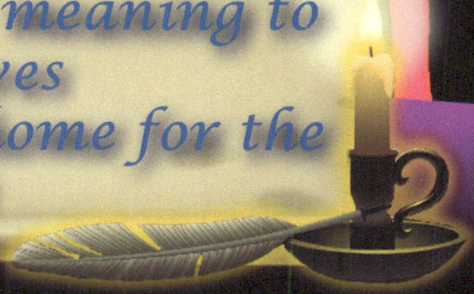

Of course, we have fun at
Christmas time
We give gifts, we visit, we
laugh
Just remember that this was
done
Long years ago on our
behalf

So eat turkey, sing carols,
Light the Christmas tree
Bake cookies, put out decorations
For all to see

*Spread joy
throughout the region
But keep clearly in mind
That Jesus is the reason
for the season*

God reached down
And touched the world
from above
It was through Jesus
He left His fingerprints of
love

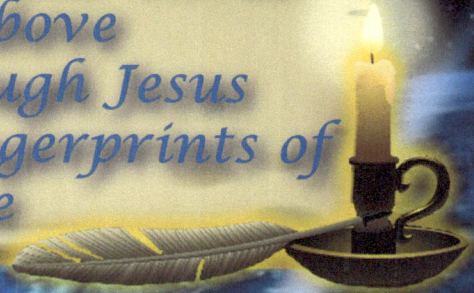

So when we say "Merry Christmas, y'all" We are really proclaiming that.....

Jesus is the best gift of all!

To: You From: Jesus with Love

Butterfly Promise

Angelina and Friends Discover the
Secret of
Who They Were Meant To Be

story by Linda Crosland
art by Malcolm Crosland

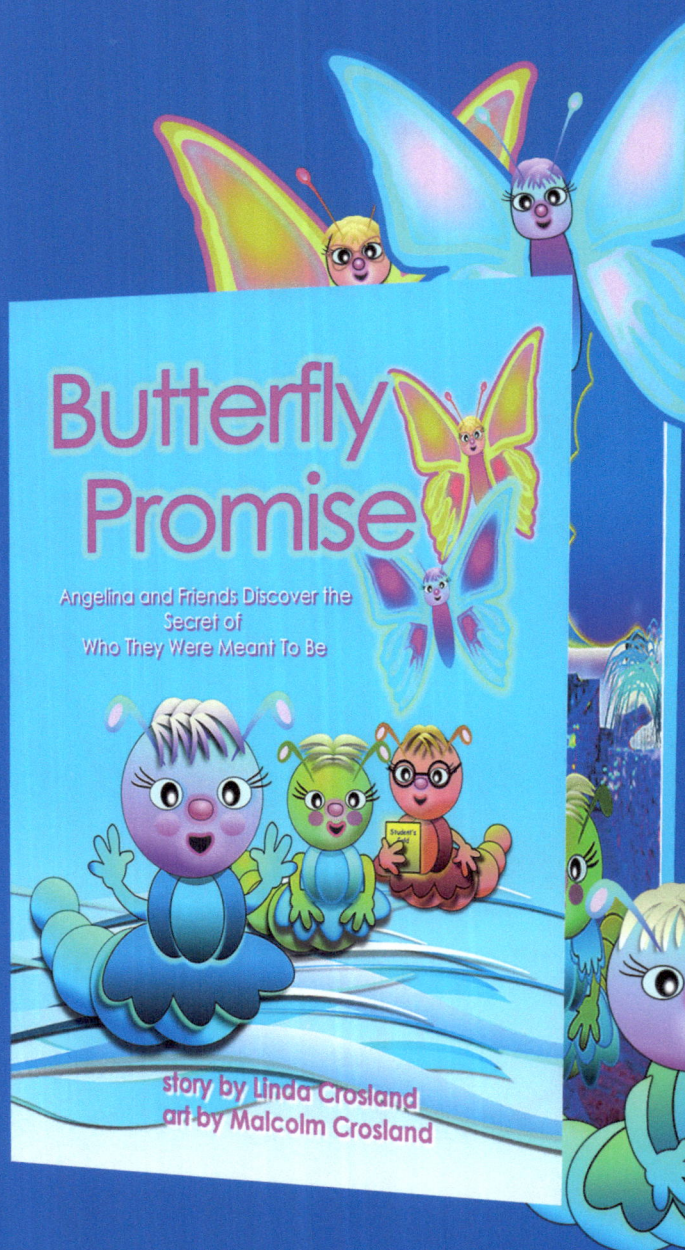

Other Books by the
Author

Butterfly Promise

Angelina and Friends
Discover the Secret
of Who They Were
Meant To Be

Author's website: lindacrosland.com

www.ingramcontent.com/pod-product-compliance
Lightning Source LLC
Chambersburg PA
CBHW042058040426
42447CB00003B/266